MAR 3 0 2018

SPACE TECH

LUNAR PROBES

by ALLAN MOREY

EPIC

BELLWETHER MEDIA • MINNEAPOLIS, MN

EPIC BOOKS are no ordinary books. They burst with intense action, high-speed heroics, and shadows of the unknown. Are you ready for an Epic adventure?

This edition first published in 2018 by Bellwether Media, Inc.

No part of this publication may be reproduced in whole or in part without written permission of the publisher. For information regarding permission, write to Bellwether Media, Inc., Attention: Permissions Department, 5357 Penn Avenue South, Minneapolis, MN 55419.

Library of Congress Cataloging-in-Publication Data

Names: Morey, Allan.
Title: Lunar Probes / by Allan Morey.
Description: Minneapolis, MN : Bellwether Media, Inc., 2018. | Series: Epic.
   Space Tech | Audience: Age 7-12. | Includes bibliographical references and index.
Identifiers: LCCN 2016057239 (print) | LCCN 2017008699 (ebook) | ISBN 9781626177024 (hardcover : alk. paper) |
   ISBN 9781681034324 (ebook) | ISBN 9781618912855 (paperback : alk. paper)
Subjects: LCSH: Lunar surface vehicles–Juvenile literature.
Classification: LCC TL480 .M67 2018 (print) | LCC TL480 (ebook) | DDC 629.43/53–dc23
LC record available at https://lccn.loc.gov/2016057239

TABLE OF CONTENTS

LUNAR PROBE AT WORK!

It is October 2009. A **NASA** lunar probe speeds toward the moon. When it lands, a cloud of **vapor** and dust rises up. This tells scientists that water may exist there. Maybe the moon can support human life!

rocket

lunar probe

LIFE ON THE MOON!

In the future, the moon
may be a base. Trips
into outer space may
start there.

WHAT IS A LUNAR PROBE?

Lunar probes are space machines that explore the moon. These probes carry lots of tools for **research**. They do not need humans with them. Their findings are sent back to scientists on Earth.

NASA scientists

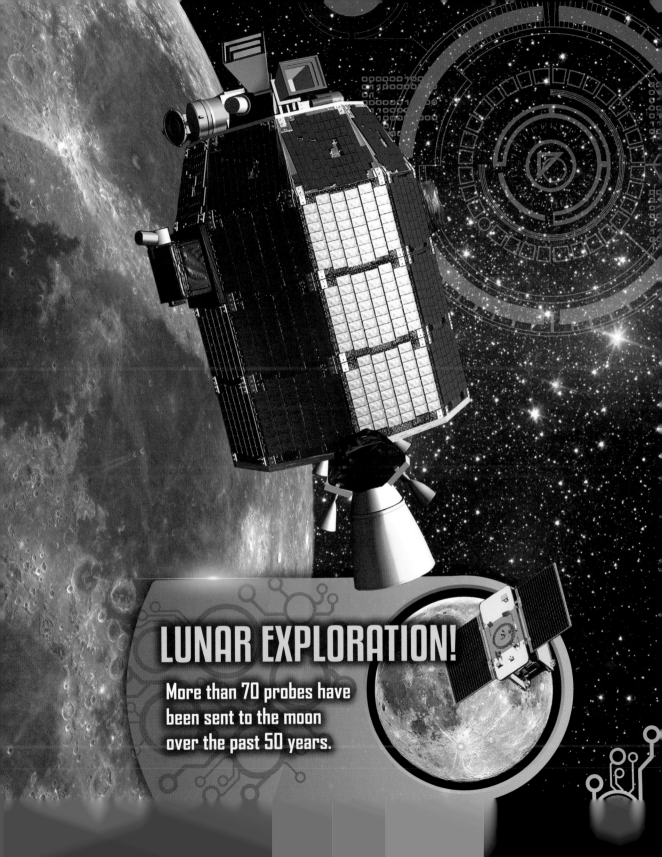

LUNAR EXPLORATION!

More than 70 probes have been sent to the moon over the past 50 years.

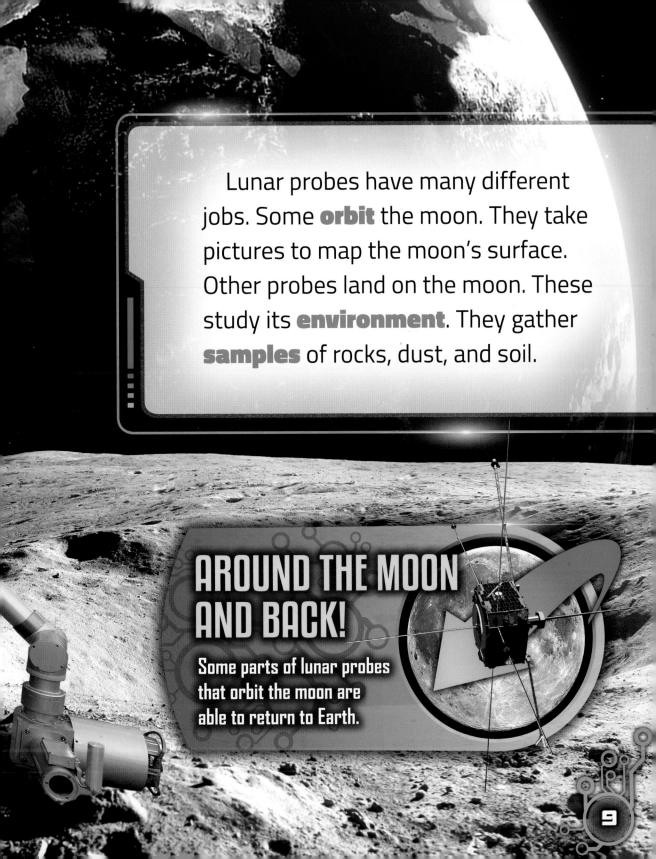

Lunar probes have many different jobs. Some **orbit** the moon. They take pictures to map the moon's surface. Other probes land on the moon. These study its **environment**. They gather **samples** of rocks, dust, and soil.

AROUND THE MOON AND BACK!

Some parts of lunar probes that orbit the moon are able to return to Earth.

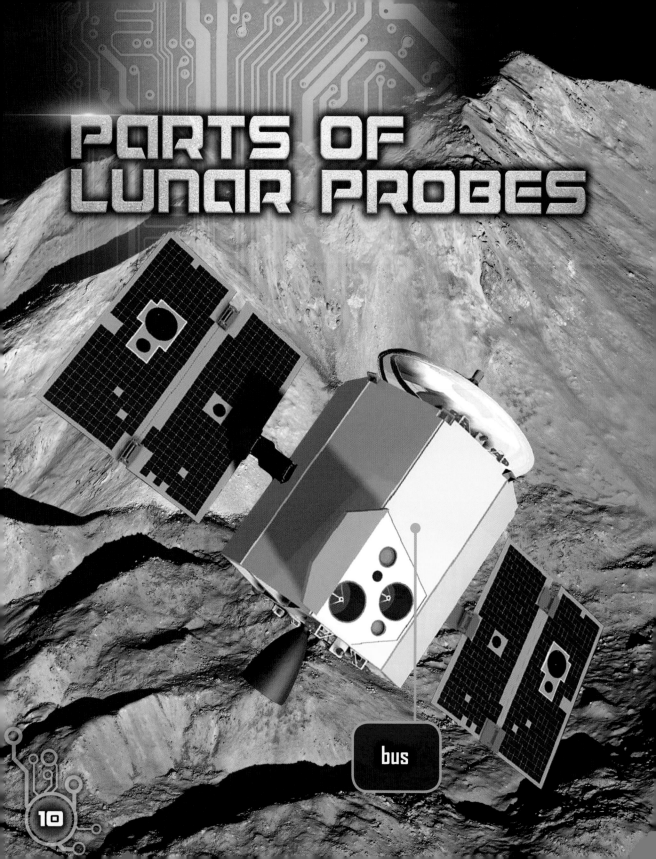

PARTS OF LUNAR PROBES

bus

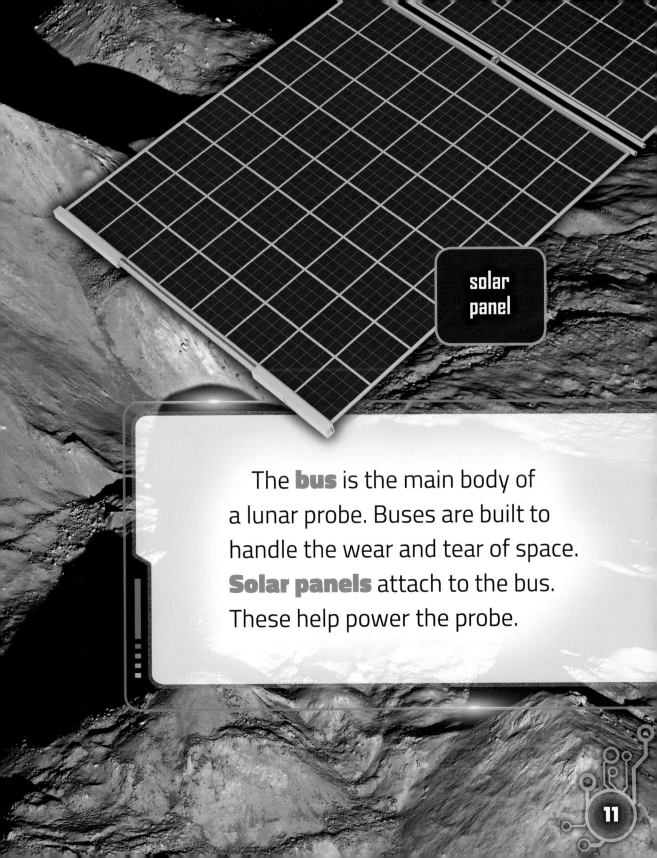

solar
panel

The **bus** is the main body of a lunar probe. Buses are built to handle the wear and tear of space. **Solar panels** attach to the bus. These help power the probe.

Buses carry the **technology** that probes need to do their jobs. Cameras snap pictures of the moon. **Sensors** measure heat and light. This information is then sent back to Earth using **radio waves**.

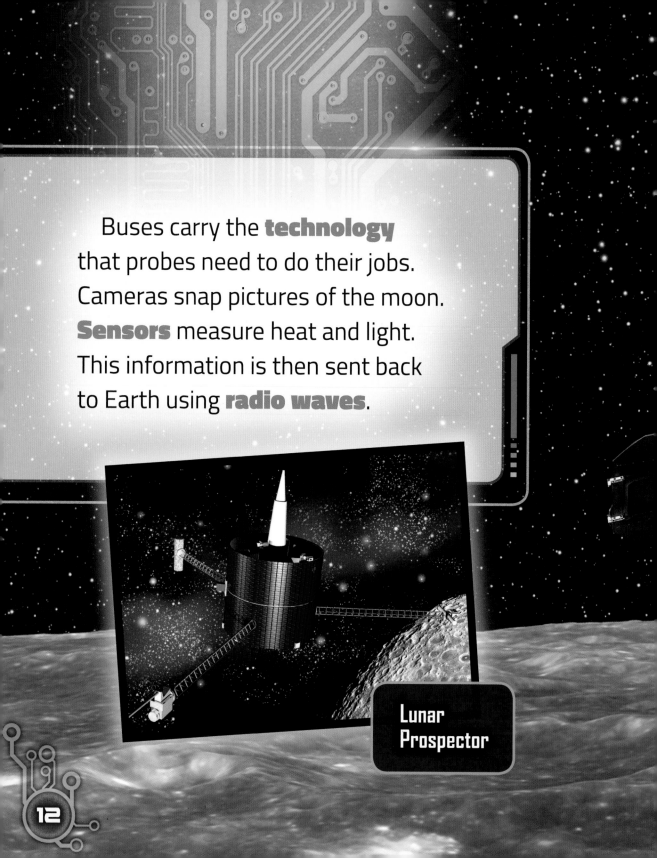

Lunar Prospector

IDENTIFY THE MACHINE

Lunar Orbiter 1

- solar panels
- bus
- scientific instruments:
  - sensors
  - cameras
  - antennae

LUNAR PROBE MISSIONS

In the 1950s, scientists began sending probes to the moon. They wanted to know what it was made of. They also wanted to know if it was safe to send people there.

Ranger probe

a lunar probe
being built

BLAST OFF!

Lunar probes are sent
into space on rockets.

orbiter

There are two types of lunar probes. **Orbiters** make maps of the moon by circling around it.

Impactors are probes that land on the moon. They study its surface and collect samples.

model of impactor

In 2009, a NASA probe found signs of water on the moon. Scientists are studying if the moon can support human life.

moon base

In the future, a **moon base** may help scientists explore further into space. Thanks to lunar probes, people may one day find a way to live on the moon!

LCROSS SATELLITE SPECS

rocket for LCROSS

LCROSS satellite

NAME: LCROSS
Lunar Crater Observation and Sensing Satellite

- **mission:** to search for signs of water on the moon
- **first time in space:** 2009

- **location in space:** Cabeus Crater on the moon

N

W   E

S

- **max speed:** 5,580 miles (8,980 kilometers) per hour

- **weight:** 1,290 pounds (585 kilograms) without fuel

- **height:** 6.6 feet (2 meters)

width: 8.6 feet (2.6 meters)

GLOSSARY

bus—the main body of a probe

environment—the characteristics of a natural area

impactors—spacecraft designed to crash-land on a planet or moon

moon base—a place on the moon that can be a center for operations or a starting point for space exploration

NASA—National Aeronautics and Space Administration; NASA is a U.S. government agency responsible for space travel and exploration.

orbit—to circle around an object

orbiters—spacecraft designed to circle around a planet or moon

radio waves—types of waves used to send information over long distances

research—to study or collect information about a subject

samples—small amounts that stand for the whole

sensors—devices used to detect things like light, heat, and sound

solar panels—devices that collect sunlight and turn it into energy

technology—any device that solves a problem

vapor—the gas form of a substance

TO LEARN MORE

AT THE LIBRARY

Bredeson, Carmen, and Marianne Dyson. *Exploring the Moon.* New York, N.Y.: Enslow Publishing, 2016.

Gifford, Clive. *Astronomy, Astronauts, and Space Exploration.* New York, N.Y.: Crabtree Publishing, 2016.

Owen, Ruth. *Probes.* New York, N.Y.: Powerkids Press, 2015.

ON THE WEB

Learning more about lunar probes is as easy as 1, 2, 3.

1. Go to www.factsurfer.com.

2. Enter "lunar probes" into the search box.

3. Click the "Surf" button and you will see a list of related web sites.

With factsurfer.com, finding more information is just a click away.

23

INDEX

The images in this book are reproduced through the courtesy of: Antonio Petrone, front cover (Earth); kvsan, front cover (moon), pp. 4-5 (moon), 6-7 (moon), 20-21 (moon), 14-15 (moon); NASA, front cover (lunar probe), pp. 5 (lunar probe/ rocket), 6 (scientists), 7 (lunar probe, lunar probe-FunFact), 9 (lunar probe-FunFact), 10-11 (lunar surface), 12 (probe), 12-13 (Earth/moon), 14 (Ranger probe), 15 (framed probe, rocket-FunFact), 19 (satellite), 20 (LCROSS rocket), 21 (LCROSS probe); Aphelleon, pp. 2-3; DM7, p. 5 (spaceship-FunFact); MarcelClemens, pp. 5 (Moon-FunFact), 7 (Moon-FunFact), 9 (Moon-FunFact); Lai xinlin - Imaginechina/ Associated Press, pp. 8-9 (lunar rover); Vadim Sadovski, pp. 8-9 (Earth/moon surface); NASA/NSSDC, p. 10 (lunar probe); Tatiana Shepeleva, p. 11 (solar panel); NASA - Langley Research Center, p. 13 (Lunar Orbiter 1); Ebs08/ Wikipedia, p. 16 (orbiter), HelenField, pp. 16-17 (lunar mountains); Himilsbah, p. 17 (rocky outcropping); LIU HUAIYU/FEATURECHINA/ Newscom, p. 17 (impactor); 3000ad, pp. 18-19 (space station); Pavel Chagochkin, pp. 18-19 (Earth/ lunar surface).